"Saints and the interface between the mystical and the human are at the heart of Sarah Law's poetry. In *This Transfigured Church of the Threads*, she steps back from the documented life of Thérèse of Lisieux and picks up phrases and ideas—the threads of the title—from her writings, to underpin these imagistic and philosophical poems. 'I write what I want to believe' says both the poet and the ventriloquized saint, in this very human, lucid book of contemplative and intriguing poems."

—RUPERT LOYDELL, author of *The Age of Destruction and Lies*

"Written with Sarah Law's usual precision and grace, these poems take us deep into the spiritual struggles and epiphanies of one of the greatest saints in modern history. Through recording the unseen moments, the unrecorded thoughts (always as fruit of long research and discernment), Law's work brings us to a marvelous closeness with Thérèse. This is poetry of quiet and extraordinary power borne of great contemplation—and it stokes great contemplation in the reader."

—SALLY READ, editor of *100 Great Catholic Poems*

"Gentle. Tender. Lovely. Sarah Law skillfully takes the reader on a quiet journey, carefully and imaginatively unfolding a life honest in its humanity but devoted to the sublime. Each profound tale of contemplative grace and longing expertly provides a glimpse of the spiritual storm inside a cloistered saint. Through Thérèse, Law draws out beauty and the divine from everyday moments—often with questioning, but always returning to love's restorative power. Read it slowly and with wonder."

—VERONICA MCDONALD, editor and founder, *Heart of Flesh Literary Journal*

"'Here in my cell I am newly conceived,' writes Sarah Law in this astonishing and absorbing meditation on the life of a beloved saint. Each poem offers a new insight on Therese's experience, and the whole book is studded with bright imagery. Law is a writer of great imaginative empathy, which she balances with formal control—her brief, graceful poems land lightly as snowflakes. These poems invite a response of both heart and mind, and reading them is a remarkable pleasure."

—**KATHRYN SIMMONDS**, author of *Scenes from Life on Earth*

This

Transfigured Chapel
of the *Threads*

This
Transfigured Chapel
of the *Threads*

Poems

by
SARAH LAW

RESOURCE *Publications* · Eugene, Oregon

THIS TRANSFIGURED CHAPEL OF THE THREADS
Poems

Resource Publications
An Imprint of Wipf and Stock Publishers
199 W. 8th Ave., Suite 3
Eugene, OR 97401

www.wipfandstock.com

PAPERBACK ISBN: 979-8-3852-0419-9
HARDCOVER ISBN: 979-8-3852-0420-5
EBOOK ISBN: 979-8-3852-0421-2

VERSION NUMBER 12/01/23

To friends far and near

Contents

Acknowledgments

Poems from this collection have appeared in:

The Bardo Group

The Be Zine

Friends Journal

Grand Little Things

Heart of Flesh

The Purpled Nail

Soul-Lit

Stride

With many thanks to the editors of these publications and to those at Wipf and Stock for their encouragement and expertise. Thank you so much to Kevin and all my family, friends and colleagues. And thank you to all the poet and writer friends I've made through *Amethyst Review*, for your ongoing support and inspiration.

Introduction: Reflecting on a Beloved Saint

Thérèse of Lisieux (1873–97) is a much-loved saint, made famous by her poignant autobiographical writing, her letters, and other creative pieces. Her brief life was lived in seclusion: she longed to be a nun from a very early age and joined the Carmelite monastery in the Normandy town of Lisieux when she was just fifteen. She died from tuberculosis nine years later, having suffered dreadful physical and spiritual trials. A wealth of information is available about her life and spirituality, as are some very moving photographs taken mostly by her own sister Céline, who also joined the Lisieux monastery, as had her two older sisters, Marie and Pauline.

All her writings are precious and have been much discussed by those with more theological and devotional insight than myself, and I have written about her life and legacy previously in both poetry and historical fiction. The idea for this collection, however, was initiated when I started to think about what is lost or missing from her work. I became increasingly interested in the idea of lost letters—of gaps and absences that elude satisfactory understanding, the tantalizing idea that spiritual and literary gleanings are hiding somewhere, just out of reach.

Thérèse herself wrote a lot of letters. Most of them are still extant and can be read as intelligently annotated, published collections, and can also be viewed in English and as the original French documents on the website of the Lisieux Carmel archives, a wonderful resource. Thérèse's letters to her sister Céline, and to the missionary seminarian correspondent of her last year, Maurice Bellière, are particularly rich in compassion and guidance. Family letters, especially those between Thérèse and her sisters, are often sweetly humorous and intimate too, so much so that there was hesitation over their initial publication. But one significant recipient throughout her life, from her pre-Carmel days until her death, was her spiritual director Père Almire Pichon (1843–1919), a Jesuit priest who had considerable spiritual sway over the whole Martin family, but who was generally absent in person from their lives, spending many years in Canada. He was a talented spiritual director and particularly astute at helping young women discern a religious vocation—something Thérèse needed no help with, although her oldest sister, Marie, did. There also seems to have been a fundamental kindness and compassion in his manner, which many of his correspondents clearly both needed and appreciated. He was a busy man, a priest, a Jesuit, a spiritual director to many souls. He was not always able to answer at length or at all to the letters sent him. His eyesight took the toll of a huge, unrelenting, correspondence. Thérèse wrote to him on a regular basis from Carmel, at least monthly, but understood how burdened he was. She wrote more as an act of discipline and self-examination than in a plea for guidance. She tended to rely on the Gospels and her own inner lights for that. But although she once declared that her whole soul was in the later letters sent to Père Pichon, we do not have a single one remaining. For his own reasons, Pichon decided to destroy the entire correspondence quite soon after Thérèse's death in 1897, and long before the cause for her canonization was initiated. It's been estimated that this correspondence comprised about a hundred letters from a young nun later declared (by Pope Pius X) 'the greatest saint of modern times'. By all accounts an inestimable loss.

The poems in this collection are not an attempt to restore what has been lost in any factual or even theological way. Instead, the concept of lost letters became for me, over several months, a sort of symbolic space for creative reflection. The epistolary poem has a long history in western poetry; a precursor to the dramatic monologue, its conventions include a concentrated use of personal voice, whether imagined or the poet's own, and it also implies a specific addressee, someone who does not reply in the poem itself.

I began by mulling over how Thérèse might have framed her thoughts, her passions and her life experiences to someone who she would at first have regarded as an authority figure, and later as more of an equal, at least in terms of suffering and religious life. The main events of Thérèse's life are well known: she pleaded with Pope Leo XIII to be allowed to enter Carmel at a young age; once she had entered, she gradually developed her profound understanding of divine love, the power of small acts, and the spiritual dimensions of both compassion and suffering. I imagined that most, if not all of these events and themes would have been present in the letters. In addition, Thérèse also had a particular affinity for the priesthood: she was fascinated by the priestly vocation, and realized during her Papal pilgrimage that priests were human as well as figures of spiritual significance, and, without any sense of sacrilege, often declared that, if born male, she would have wanted to be a priest herself. I reflected on how her knowledge of Pichon's life might have informed her meditations on and, to some extent, identification with the priesthood. Then there are the sustained notes both of poignancy and of inventive playfulness that I find throughout Thérèse's life: I wondered how they would be represented in these letters long lost to history.

I started to write short poems, and sometimes even shorter prose fragments. Thérèse is associated with littleness, and I wanted my letter-poems to reflect this. The idea came to me to write a hundred. I continued with a mixed sense of trepidation and creative play. As I wrote, I sometimes felt I was close to the spirit of Thérèse. I borrowed some of her images as well as her experiences. At other times I was more aware of my own language and perspectives finding their way into the poems. Writing poetry in the form of lost letters is bound to be an act of creative projection rather than biographical recovery: I would never pretend otherwise. In some ways I was writing *to* Thérèse as much as writing *through* her. Nonetheless, I felt the project gathered a momentum that I wanted to honor, so I often wrote nightly, hoping to draw the threads into a sustained sequence. Dwelling in this poetic chapel became part of my spiritual and creative discipline.

Our recent global pandemic has had an impact on the writing of these poems and on my own perception of life in Carmel in Thérèse's time. A world of strict enclosure, a world where health could not be taken for granted and where fatal respiratory infection could suddenly sweep through a community: all became frighteningly real to many during months of lockdown and for some, illness. Like many, I became intensely aware of life's fragility, even as I found myself more drawn to prayer and simple trust than ever before. I wondered how Thérèse would see such a situation, and I realized how closely she lived out her restricted life of enclosure in the context of ubiquitous mortality. I also came to believe that she would view the pandemic not as some kind of chastisement, but as yet another lesson in how to love. My essential understanding of Thérèse is that she saw everything in that way. She was a student of love, and the harder the lesson, the more determined she was to learn it and put it into action for the rest of her life and beyond. I have tried to explore this idea, no doubt inadequately, in my poems too. I hope the following poems provide some food for thought on language, on transfiguring grace, and perhaps on Thérèse herself.

Sarah Law

This
Transfigured Chapel
of the Threads

1

Mon Père, I thank you for your blessing—
in this crawlspace between bed and wall

I count it with my precious things;
among blue marbles, holy cards, a doll

with a pink sash, a water vial
into which I dip my finger, scribing

a sign with invisible ink into the air.
Down and across—I consecrate it all,

and promise to remember you in prayer,
the little droplets gleaming as they fall.

2

I have said the *Memorare* fifty-two times,
the *Confiteor* twenty, and wondered how

so small a Child could have so large a heart,
and how his mother, brim-full of worry,

could trust that her world would be pressed
like grapes into fine wine. I have drawn

and polished the pearls from my first retreat,
tested the toughness of my little boat,

and—with your permission—wait to be launched
from the shore into sun-shot waters.

3

You know I am the youngest of us all. I hold
my hands before me as a pledge; my fingers

point upwards, like the Carmel's chapel tower;
my little bones are family, the tips the littlest—

and yet they are the highest, reaching neatly
to the heavens. My soul's the small witness

of the tendons and the sinews and the joints;
I stretch myself up on the bare convent roof—

lightning may strike, and the rain lash out;
the mist and morning dew surround me.

4

Your hands lift God at the altar:
white fire dwelling in a disc;

what is this calling of lightning conductor—
to be electrified, so that one touch

can charge a city? Here I play papers
and dolls, rendering all my toys

disposed to gathering grace,
and here is a strand of my hair—

see how the thunder allows it to rise;
hectic, bright, defying gravity.

5

I dreamt of Jesus on the cross
and that I had knelt down to him,

I heard the struggling lungs, I saw
the drops of blood and water,

I knew of his agony, caught between
God and nothingness. When I looked up

with my fingers clasped and my heart
struggling with love's thick clot—

I saw how his hands had slipped
from their nails, his arms cradling the air

as though my offering had gifted him
with the whole hurting world.

6

I loved learning as a child, but not the tattle-filled classes. To sit in a nook at home, to turn the pages of history, oh! Time is a rolled-out song. On, onwards, I think, to wield the scythe of science—its drops and drugs, the running engine's gleam. Soon we will fly, I tell the maid; she knuckles her hips and snorts. I gave her the medal you blessed, thinking to please her. I grip my rosary then, and closing my eyes, imagine a mother's rush: the curve and grasp of her arms, the severing blade that cradles and draws us, limping, into the infinite.

7

I twist my blonde hair up into
an infinity loop, restrained with pins,

it sits, a knotted nest, upon my head.
I fasten my neck-high dress. I clip

my belt, pull in my waist, sit tight
for the bishop to beckon me in

to his lush dark parlor. *And what
do you wish for?* Only this: the rough-

spun robe, the gem-bright grass,
the freedom of finality.

8

That tunnel through the mountain,
its black rush, crash of sound—

O my father, is this head-on death?
I have hankered after martyrdom,

the drama of severance, and yet
the sheer void, the long-drawn

clamor of hollowed-out rock—
a nothingness I had not intimated,

nor had I prepared for the shock
of hurtling back into the light.

9

What is a priest? a little chip of white
close to the throat. A long black swish

like a shadow, or a shored-up barque
at the harbor's edge. A further father

berthing souls in silence. Even a father
can mother us. But a father can still lose

his purpose. What I see on pilgrimage
are fathers jousting with the *mise-en-scène,*

their ragged standards flutter in the weather
while my sails are full of dreams.

10

If I had been another sort of child,
how would I have fared in the world?

A girl who danced the quadrilles,
and swayed her hips to keep the hoop

encircling her waist—who bit her lips
and pinched her cheeks to redden them,

who met the young man's gaze
when he helped her from her carriage;

who did not have a seal upon her heart—
pledged to the Word in marriage.

11

Old man with his shock of white—
white robes, white hair, blenched

skin and halo *sans* glare, this Pope,
nearly fallen like a fruit from his own life—

I know my lines and the fall to my knees,
my face pale under the dark mantilla, *O*

let me go, I'll plead, *let me go in*. Just
his nod would be enough, the raised hand

imparting permission. Denied, I'll be dragged
away with my one wild petition.

12

Patience grinds this crumb
into its glassy self:

a sugar crystal
on a poor girl's tongue,

a grain of luxury
in cold skim milk;

a treat for a pet,
the prioress's cat—

my own soul thirsty
for a word.

13

I recovered my belt-buckle at the last minute,
scrabbling in the rubble at the side of the church

but oh! my coach was gone, and only one—
Monsignor's wealthy coterie—remained.

Obliged, I took my place like some lost soul,
clutching her broken halo in her arms.

I write to you calmly. At the time, I begged
my guardian angels give my words wings.

Sunlight gleamed into our rolling world,
and made a miracle of rescued things.

14

Things I have seen in lucid dreams:
a face in the fine lace curtains;

a loaf in the shape of a church; crumbs
and seeds like eyes, rolling and blinking

into my palm's fresh field.
Pint-sized demons with flatiron feet

skittering from my gaze.
A bright heart scribbled in the sky,

a father figure hidden by a veil,
a woman with her arms raised high.

15

I practice in the Carmel of the home,
sit prim with your letter on my lap,

and when the clock chimes, I fold up
into a thin paper sister, a flimsy fan

for love's great heat. The others say *live
just a little; sweet raisins are hidden*

in gateaux and brioches; take, eat!
I smile. Consider the riches of prayer—

I'm gathering grains of sugar and rice;
the hearth's breath rattles and scatters.

16

Here are my sins, *Mon Père*, on
the eve of my postulancy: I

have taken pleasure in a satin ribbon,
the sharp scent of *eau-de-cologne*;

been proud: of my lustrous hair,
my own bare arms; felt anger

at my classmates for their roughness,
and my sisters for their polish;

harbored envy for the martyred—
insisted on forgiveness like the sun.

17

It took some time, *Mon Père*, before my pulse returned to normal.
Perhaps, having taken vows yourself, you understand. But to walk
through a door into the gauzy dawn—to leave all you know, only
to sense a familiar whisper within veiled forms—

Here, living and waiting converge into a further world. Here in my
cell I am newly conceived. The soul grows in seclusion; the senses
discerning a heartbeat so much stronger than my own.

18

Things I have found and adored:
the dust that dances in the oratory;

the ink of the night sky, its shifting clouds;
the unexpected blessing of the snow,

yes, but also the rain's fat drops, the
sunshine poured like golden honey

on my body as I kneel alone.
The dregs and scrapes of paint I use

to make the mundane holy, knowing now,
as I do, that it already is.

19

I have retrieved, *Mon Père*, the grace
of clumsiness. Just now I dropped

my copybook: its cracked spine
fractured all my limping words;

earlier I knocked the bread
from basket to refectory floor;

for penance, I wear broken crusts
around my neck. I think of them

as sacramental; rough-cut hosts—
and I their battered chalice.

20

In the morning I raise my hands to the sky. The dawn is glimmering at its base, honey in a glass, waiting to be stirred, to diffuse its own sweetness. I make a frame with forefingers and thumb. A neat picture, smaller and humbler than my artist sister. Yet the blue intensifies, the clouds swell and disperse, and I wait for the sun's softening power.

In the evening I cup my hands. They are empty and open enough to receive the day's breath, to be held like a smile before the shutting of a door.

21

When I was young my sister gifted me
with a toy pistol. I was terrified,

and begged Papa to take the gun away –
I was no boy to play the games of war!

But now I dream of battlefields—
my sword, a slice of light, always at hand

to the point of martyrdom. While
I wait for my commission, I

am drunk on fighting spirit—and
the warrior's vocation that comes with it.

22

Sometimes fake flowers are a kindness; *mock* the description is gentle; *mock* as a verb has a bittersweet sting. I arrange tissue lilies and cornflowers around the Child's feet; himself an imitation of our living Divinity. An old sister comes up shaking her head. She thinks to scold me for causing her fever.

I seek to save her dignity and pluck three petals from their paper cluster. 'So clever, what we can make these days.' I give her my best smile.

She responds with a brief bloom of friendship. Its scent remains with me; I scrunch up my sacrificed tokens.

The cloister walk's flagstones are dappled with grace.

23

To sit in the choir, in silence—the mouth full of silence, the hands open, palms up; silence pouring down. Silence casts harmonics in the body—ears veiled from word and world. The night office is pooled in solemn hush. But silence is not dark: it is more like a mist; the plume of a breath in a background of snow. Silence is a white haze blooming over water. I sit in my stall. My soul unfurls along life's ticking river.

24

I have found gold
in the sunlight, gold
in the hay; the priest's bright stole
and gold in his hair, the
aureole of slender mother and child;
gold paint (my fingers
gilded with its dust):

I hold the chalice. It reflects
my face transposed
into a pure gold curve.

25

Here are my faults, *Mon Père,*
on the eve of my veiling:

I have shivered in the washhouse,
lingered in the cloister with my broom;

been stubborn with my mothers
(I considered them imposters), slipped

away from the gaze of slowcoach sisters,
hugged myself under the covers—

forgive me all these minor spills—
I should have spilled myself.

26

Like a bird in a cage or a mouse in a box, O Father, I am struggling with limits. The only way is under, to duck the head, and slip into a nook. Water is a luxury. Heaven is a luxury, an exuberance of giving. There's nothing economical about it. Grace is a gift, drifting down onto the bed like dust.

27

As a girl I would stare—
at the light

       creeping slow
as the slow hand's sway,

sense the spirits of my lost
little siblings
       hanker after wings

now,
a woman covered in my calling,
the light is still
       glowing,
       a moon-pure clockface,
a spyhole, an aperture, in whom, and
with whom, and through whom
I am

beheld. I write

to you, as I let my breath unfurl
onto the mantle of the world.

28

When the child came,
I lifted him high—his baby-blond hair
is my own, his christening gown

cut down from my own wedding dress.
He was silent. The weight of him
feathery light, yet heavy

as a world. O mothers
who fan out beside me, recursive
as whispers, his message is clear,

I have made myself little and infinite,
take me to heart—
there is nothing to fear.

29

I am told that sleep is sin (outside
the rule of dark night hours on

my mattress, roughly stuffed with hay)—
illicit sleep caresses me at prayer,

the choir stalls soften with its kisses,
I let my head droop in sleep's warmth,

O dove breast, O loosening blood—
I am drunk, just a little, with pleasure

at the solving of my body, at
this offering of everything at once.

30

Here are my sins, *Mon Père,*
on the eve of my profession:

I have bothered the novices
with my eager words; lost

time in the meadow's soft grass,
gossiped in the courtyard, been

caught drowsing at Matins,
browsing glossy fashion in my cell—

tracing patterns with my little pencil
and finding them beautiful.

31

There is a science to falling upwards—
one takes the marrow of a life, titrates

its goodness into little beads; threading
them on steel so strong the hands

of night could not prevail. Prayer is
a mother scooping up her child

behind glass doors; and elevating her.
Anyone can trip and go flying—catch

the pendant heart, gleaming
like an *Amen* as it spreads and lifts.

32

I have found a little oratory in my heart, *Mon Père*. I painted the walls in living colors; velvet dark, rainbow bright. I bring bunches of wildflowers and fill the small place with scent. In the day (eyes lowered), I visit my inner chapel, like a Russian doll who holds all her daughters within her: it seems to me the dimensions of this life are slender walls through which a soul—a simple soul—may slip. Even in the night, I dream myself there.

Let us kneel before this altar, on which sits a Child with hands outstretched.

33

I have not used the discipline
Mon Père, for many months;

its whip of knotted cords lies
discarded in the corner. Nor

did I long bear the sharp iron cross—
my flesh only worried and wept

where I could have felt peace.
I understand fire is a hazardous yearning—

still, I would offer my whole self
to stop the world burning.

34

I have discovered love skews gravity—
the weight with which I smooth a sheet

when moved by love's immeasurable—
with the mere dip of a spoon I make waves

raised and rushing up to God. An eyelid's
flicker, chanting Latin psalms,

casts love's ripples into hurting souls
and those outside the shadow of a dream;

how my struggling breath mists up dark
glass into the mercy of dawn.

35

Carmelites are busy bees. Here in the hive, we make honey from sunshine and prayer. Look how my limpid window waits—like us, she says the hours, and some of those hours prove more than golden. O Father—this window is purer than I: she does not eat, she does not gossip; if she sleeps, I do not see her. When she sheds her tears, she remains at peace within. I sit with her on my clumsy kneeler, wait to be touched by her clarifying grace. The honey I've spun with her help is the sweetest.

Tincture of time and place; witness of crystal; enduring taste. Thus, I can offer you sustenance—you at the table where the air is cold, the bread is bitter.

36

With all my clumsy sentences and songs
I hope to make you smile, *Mon Père*,

the way a child delights her mother's heart,
or a poor girl, given fine sandwiches

dreams against the tree, while Papa casts
for the *bon mot*, a flash of fish—

it seems I have one bouquet I can share,
the holy moment of the lips and eyes

as though I tender in my catch of time
a little sliver of eternity.

37

In answer to your question: yes, I feel the cold. It seeps in, sets the bones into stiff poses. My feet and fingers burn and freeze. Alone, I wrinkle my nose, and am too cold to feel my face return to peace. Then I am contrite, imagining angels at my elbows, serene and composed. *Mère* Marie has given me a heater: I lift my bare soles over its glow. Warmth returns as my chilled flesh thaws; heat suffusing my skin like grace. This reclamation of pleasure is, briefly, painful. A redemption of the body, imparting its own hope.

38

Our founding mother bid us keep
his picture. I think often of

his face, love's burning death-mask
after sacrifice. All passion spent,

his bruised lips pressed together,
the blood-beads fallen from his crown

of thorns have formed dark diamonds
in this portrait caught on holy cloth.

My heart adheres to his imprint.
His eyes are closed. I dare not blink.

39

We have been raking the hay in our meadow, *Mon Père*. You may remember it, the size of a pocket handkerchief—yet Céline's photograph renders it a vast expanse. The sunshine blesses us, is sweet as honey; the hay is sweet and light; the sisters smile. I am struck with a sudden sense of heaven: this meadow in the sun; the golden racks of hay; God's delight at his ongoing harvest of souls.

40

I am learning the art of the love-note,
brief lines kindling a glow,

paper wings folded in pockets, slipped
under cell-doors or tucked into books,

and, knowing words alone won't hold
my weight or catch my light, my pencil

makes its marks—an underscore, full
of insistence, or passion, or wit—

the toppled dazzle of a candle
when my heart would take her flight!

41

Disease spreads her wings like a black moth over our mortal community. As a student of love, I will not fear her. Every ragged flutter is a puzzle for love to resolve. The conundrum is that love is both method and answer, a cool clean cloth to the fevered brow.

Mon Père, disease casts a harsh shadow—but look at the waves of light gathering in her wake.

42

I am just a little brush —
fine-haired, slim-tipped,
made to amend a smudge
with my whitening touch,
just a tiny hand—I
follow the outlines,
barely look beyond them.
Yet this discipline
has been a gift to me,
and when I lift my fingers
to your brow, it is to add
my dab of light.

43

I see the faces of my novices, each a smudge of grace in the dark work of my days. One is a slender girl given to tears—I open my hand and proffer her a shell. "Weep only here," I tell her. She lifts the shell's lip to her cheek and lets herself laugh. Another is a scared soul, scarred in ways I cannot fathom. "Come," I say, "You are under the care of a King." Then I have my own sullen sister, blazing with art. I struggle to hold her faith to a fire that eyes cannot see, nor the heart fully feel. I imagine myself as a pastor, grasping a staff and a handful of wool.

44

Since old and useless things are stowed
up in the convent loft, I wondered

whether they were nearer heaven
than our bustling nuns below—

perhaps the chill preserves them;
humility is fostered in the dark.

I crept up in my clumsy sandals,
touched rough wood, cracked bowls,

and honored their abandonment—
my hands made holy with dust.

45

God comes to me in daily irritants:
a tepid splash of dirty laundry water,
a cobweb resolute against my cloth,
a snag of fishbone in the meagre soup,
my reticence interpreted as sloth;
the cough and scrape of sisters in the choir,
a finger-smudge on cards I have designed,
a blanket gone. No room beside the fire.
A streak of pain. A faith I cannot find:
I welcome everything as bread and wine.

46

I am guilty of the pleasures of the page, *Mon Père*. I let my words decorate these pure gray lines, little lace trails frothing up a dress. Train tracks. Altar rails. Ears and tails pressing their letters together. I pen my poems when sisters commission it; all is assignment under our threefold vow. The tracks of time between supper and Compline are full of silent language, spit-polished children, swinging their legs from the wire.

Pray indulge me, let me know when I should stop.

47

My sister misses you, *Mon Père*. She waits
for your words as flowers do rain, braced

for too-harsh pellets, or their arid lack,
hopes for love's soft patter, letters

of her name scribed by your hand,
pages that sail here just as you yourself

do not. For me, your silence does me good,
the longer absence pools between us

the sweeter it grows—the stronger
do I sense the soothing darkness of the sky.

48

Here are my mortifications, *Mon Père*:
custody of the eyes; sustained
contemplation of dusty cloister tiles;

the scratch of nail on tooth that scrapes
faith's skin—cracked seeds muddle my heart
until I let them in to bed and bloom;

the damp mold of the step; the acrid
steam of the wash house, the fetid
pain seeping from infirmary windows;

the touch of nothing in the night. The slow
failure of my rosary, the cold
of the water, and the stones, and the stairs

are my nightly struggle. The wormwood
I sprinkle over the smear of my meals.
The salt of my own surging blood.

49

Here are the miracles
I have witnessed, *Mon Père*:

a mother, extending
her small white hands;

a fillip of grace
in a darkened land,

the delicate lace
of the falling snows

and the scent
of the unpetalled rose.

50

For half the day there is no sun. For half a life, perhaps, a soul must dwell without it. Where then is the grace? In a candle's kiss—all light is reduced to a flickering aureole. I have seen with my own eyes how the sun's flame blooms from one dark wick.

51

Hidden in the universe
a planet—

huddled on the planet,
many lands—

thin places
hidden in the cities—

inner space hosting
hidden work—

lowered eyes
seeking hidden light—

hidden hands
clasped under habits—

the soul's tryst
with a hidden God.

52

Pictures I have painted:
a house in a black and white meadow,

a girl with a bonnet of flowers
(eyes shut tight and collar high),

a man with outstretched arms, waiting
at a platform as the girl's foot

                                        hovers
                dissipating crowds

an infant smiling in his sleep,
an old man sitting on a throne,

a grown man knocking at an unmarked door
for which there is no handle.

53

He accepts our worship, the patterns of our days, like the shadowy hulk of a chapel. Made so that light pours through the glass and gaps; shines like eternity into time's interstices (we souls gathered inside).

My sister takes her photographic negatives; each face is a smudge surprised by a halo—so a structure only serves to frame an unearned grace. Such is my thought, my confessor. Through loosening our gaze, we find this picture hidden in plain sight. It is everywhere and cannot be pinned down.

54

How hard it is to pray the rosary. I imagine myself trying to juggle precious eggs, only to drop them when I should be touching, catching and looping all my *Aves* through the air. How I struggle to balance my words, my pictures, my praise. Yet here I am like a child in the temple. Inside the hard shell of ritual, the soft heart of God. Studding the cool chains of reason, the pleasure of love. Inside all scholarship, play. Inside my suffering, joy.

55

I am under the protection of a queen, but I care more for her cloak than her crown, *Mon Père*. She hides us just as she hid herself. There is a softness to the cloth, a night-time darkness.

She was unafraid of being abandoned, wrapping her cloak about her heart. When I was lost, she taught me to smile.

She gathers us up and calls for wine.

56

At Matins I saw that our God is not a god of reckoning. He does not care to count our debts and failings. Love is so much gold ink spilled across the ledger.

57

Sleep is a syrup fed me in spoonfuls. I am given draughts in the choir—my guardian angel appears in the shafts of sunlight, holding the golden bottle aloft. I wake, falling, sometimes fallen. A slumbering novice. I push myself further down in penance. I do not feel guilt.

Sleep hides under the bed's bare slats as the cold of the night sets in.

I cannot begrudge the sleeping of others. Even my love, sleeping on in his boat as the storm swells near. I would creep into his arms as the warm dream of a child, or a sword's nestled edge.

58

There are no walls in my dreams, *Mon Père*; only meadows. Archways, yes, as decorative epitaphs, yearning high—but no boundaries, no dank divisive chapters. Instead, every meadow has its spread of tapestries.

Somewhere there is a drawing of me, lost to spots of color at my feet, to the soft meadow-grass, the glow of the setting sun.

59

Please, rest your eyes, *Mon Père*.
I understand your weariness,

scrutinizing letters plenteous
as falling leaves. In their veins

are whispered women's wishes;
on their hand-span of paper,

our sacrificial sighs. Holding
each missive with your fingers

you will sense us—the dry heat
of scruples. The empty blue skies.

60

I peel back belief like the rings of an onion, brush covert tears with the back of one hand while clasping my knife in the other. The creeds and the councils are so many layers to prize and slide away: they drop like crescent moons into a bucket. The new living surface is soft to the touch. I unwind it nevertheless, slip under the wrappings of language to something dearer still. I will cherish whatever is there—a white nub of nothing, an atom, a pearl—knowing it is good news, trusting it is gift.

61

When the dawn came, I looked at the cloth
and saw it was blood. A tidemark
after last night's hot salt rush.

I see in it stars and irregular blooms,
a country I cannot identify, though you
may know it. I see a coming flood.

There is an elation in knowing my death
is shaped like a savior seeking me,
commissioned to bring me home.

Annunciation—like the sudden sun
that shafts down from dark clouds:
searing and then gone.

62

There is a sister, seventeen years my senior, whose soul excels in scratching mine. I hold her especially dear, knowing how a harsh surface polishes while softer touches leave little shine. Just as a shadow was rising in my mouth, she offered me luminous fruit: her dream of an empty room, where I dress in fine clothes before a large black door. I told her how little hope I have in heaven, that I fear to blaspheme when I fail to believe. But slim white lines frame faith's shut shape: they press and gleam against my blocked-up sight.

63

I offer you apologies, *Mon Père*, for
today I have to write to you of nothing,

the nothing life of penitence and prayer,
the nothings of the recreation hall, where

sometimes I have acted out my nothings
to no critical acclaim. The nothing mornings

when my head is as a void. The never-
ending trial of nothing-ever-comes—ah, not

until belief has come to utter nothing
will I start to understand.

64

It is a long journey. The travails of the heart—its rested seed becomes a rooted longing to go on.

65

Mon Père, I could have been a missionary:
heat bearing down on my vulnerable skin,

offering only love in place of sin—
love cupped like petals in my hands,

soft as a cloud or a new-born lamb,
then (love set free) I'd make the shape

of emptiness fulfilled by its own rhythm,
a cross between river and waterfall,

and pour out love, to quench and rinse—
world-wide and vertical.

66

I wonder, *Mon Père*, if you have a patron saint. I imagine a Francis de Sales, lifting sad souls with his gentle words—or are you the other St Francis, calling us home like a flock of lost birds? I think of you too as St Ignatius, soldiering on with a tear in his eye.

As for me—I am no great Mother, speared by an angel; mapping her vast inner castle. No: I am dark-eyed Joan, a young girl called against all reason, wielding a sword and serving even as she burned; I am Théophane, caged and singing—all for love I have not earned.

67

Things I have broken or lost:
A fur-lined slipper and a water-jug,

a pencil stub. A rusty iron cross
uselessly pushed inside my scapular;

old rosary beads; already loose
within the chain that held them.

A wick from a cracked lamp; a
slender needle, and a reel of thread;

now falling from my fingers is all sense
of a good end—I fear that faith has fled.

68

There is only so much time,
there is only so much faith,

there is only so much laughter,
and only so much breath.

I can only pray so much,
I can never do enough,

we are limited in hours,
diminishing in power—

yet my little heart is charged
with so much love—

69

I have found God in the linen room,
within stiff folds of serge, and the tough

pleats of bodies asked to bear
their own spoiled fabric. I have raised

the sheets in thin cool air; aligned
the corners thumb to finger, stepped

with arms outstretched like Mary
visiting Elizabeth. So, Father,

we are gathered up together—in this
transfigured chapel of threads.

70

All hearts are sacred, even those despoiled by blotch and shadow. Oh, Father, do you not see us, faces veiled but hearts exposed and flaming?

Let us imitate our God who opens the gates of his body and ushers us in. Everything necessary, everything lovely is kindled at this core.

The more sacred the heart, the more like the sun: God's hearth a blaze on which I cannot look—nor look away.

71

I hold my courtyard pose for nine
long seconds, while Céline attends the lens—

fever shivering my marrow; patience
near its end. *Your portrait's formed*

in darkness: Céline straightens up,
not knowing how entirely she describes me,

how falling short—of decades and of breath—
informs my whole experience, and how

a final faltering surrounds me, as I look
for a light in the time that's left.

72

I must whisper that some books have it wrong, *Mon Père*. It is not God's pent-up vengeance on our sins that causes him to cry out loud. The lightning that electrifies the night is neither anger nor despair. And yet, God is gravid with love. She only wants my waiting hands for her waters to break and pour.

I dare to take my baby steps into the torrent, becoming love's channel as my own banks burst.

73

My convictions slip like shadows
over shifting sand. We had news of a girl

who suffered in a cult and was set free—
I had thought I could reach her with words

and I thought she had answered me,
but then her name dissolved into a stain

on a hall's cracked wall. My faith
was dragged like hers into mockery; now

I fasten the shadows tight—
bowing my head under dark stars.

74

He takes me as a mercy; on earth I'm denied the sacrament I most desire; not of marriage—I have that, mystically, in this lucent house—but of priestly ordination. Twenty-four years is the minimum age; the hours of one day and the years of my life. Imagine I have studied, immersed myself in litany and language; imagine I have wings, am transfigured by the bishop's blessed hands; imagine I am man.

You know I am happily mortal, a fragment. Imagine—I am priested just as I am.

75

Mon Père, I would send you a keepsake;
a clipping of hair or a pearly crescent

of fingernail; a sliver of skin or bone,
an eyelash-comma, a squat-root tooth,

salt drops of water or blood released
from my body's half-torn envelope—

I would distil myself into a mist,
condense and settle on your metal

crucifix; your own hands, as they hold
this little letter to the light.

76

Even the air is sacred, O Father—this gift so intimate that we are sustained by what we hardly notice. The fire, the earth, water in the stoup, all are blessed as sacramentals, and each of the elements has its station and symbol and function. The tiniest flame; the dew of the *asperges*. The handful of earth on the hard-oak coffin. But air— who can apportion it? It rolls itself out unstintingly; we're filled with as much as we can bear.

I stand in the cloister, inhaling the star-filled night. I cough for the doctor, distracting him from God's transparency. He leaves me toys—a ball in a spiral cone—to strengthen my struggling lungs. The ball is caught and buoyant in the gust of a nurse's breath. But breathing is no game—each sip is a raw-edged effort, a forced *credo*, an act of the will.

I turn the page in my copybook. Each slip of the paper's a sigh, an expiration.

77

My nurse has pushed my bed before the window
to sweeten the lessening scene of my days—

sunlight dapples the grass as the garden stretches
into meadow, and the gleam of chestnut leaves;

birds dance, hopeful for scraps, then vanish
with airborne ease. The slow bloom of the roses

is as steadfast as our faith. Except, in faith,
I struggle to keep my gaze on nature's canvas,

drawn, ever more as I am, to the shadows—
the small dark archway of the hermitage.

78

Last night I dreamt I was a bird with petals for feathers. I took off from the window ledge and flew towards the sun, shedding myself utterly.

79

If heaven is a fortune, I will spend it—
scatter God's infinite matter like water,

let it shower down and quench
the parched world. If heaven is a flower

I will cast its petals over your wounds,
the satin-soft touch of my fingers

pattering their letters like a teacher
on her unseeing student; our lives

are full of love's winged currency, and I
will show you a face made dear with dew.

80

We all have a tincture of thievery about us. I take a taste of sauce, dipping my finger into the bowl. I overhear a joke and snatch it to sell as my own. By our weakness we are obliged to take a bite, a break, a view. None of it is ours by rights.

It's as hard to accept the world as gift—none of it earned, all of it priceless—as it is to give from the city of the self. Here, the shelves stacked with my days. Here, the wildlife. Here the flamey treasure.

The method I have learned is to steal and win Him round. The next step is to leave the self unlocked. The final prize is this: I open my door for the Thief: I am His for the taking.

He will recognize me, one of His own.

81

Here are my prayer intentions
as I reach the summer's end:

the lost, slipped from their calling
like a spaniel from a lead;

those who conjure phantoms
in the hope that truth will yield;

the misfits and the starving
at the barren picnic bench;

for my own small soul to bear
its mission in the firmament.

82

Here are the souls, *Mon Père*,
God has led me to nurture:

a man who murdered and lost
his heart and head but held his soul;

another who left the priesthood
to marry and worry the unsaved world;

a fraudster who conjured a woman,
the woman who furthered his plan;

an unknown soldier, praying
in a burning fatherland.

83

I start to see a parallel, *Mon Père*
in your absence, prolonged over these years,

and the silence in my soul; God is a groom
departed, leaving me, His bride, bereft.

You are half a world away, and I have learned
that a priest not only represents Our Lord,

but imitates Him even with his distance. I still wait,
(consoled by this: my sitting in the dark

means God is always dwelling in the light)
wrapped in my mantle of abandonment.

84

I have no faith in medicine, *Mon Père*,
and yet I would like to have healed

this world's broken soldiers—
to have bound their wounds with cloth

stripped from my habit, held my folded
veil against the hemorrhaging dark.

Most of all I would have touched
my fingers to the frail skin of a pulse,

and afterwards prescribed a cordial—
signed with my doctor's cross.

85

These last weeks I have studied the theology of coughing. An impulse, an instinct, a compulsion—this animal noise, the un-remitting bark of the self. How can a guttural cry be grace? The coughed-up offering is not a community act. And yet it is: my sisters wait at the gate with me; I am the passenger, gripping my ticket; each cough is a puff from God's fast-approaching train.

86

I am alone, *Mon Père,*
in this liminal state.

My years blink out
like dying stars, and still

black water will not rise
over my head. I

shall breathe for as long
as she wants me to—

the air filling my lungs
like a persistent mother bird.

87

I have written to my missionary brother, *Mon Père*. His soul is dry, like mine, and all the more flammable for that. I wondered, as I folded my paper: can prayer be like a match? A thin line striking at the roughened heart—would that I could catch the light in the small lens of my words.

88

I do not struggle for my faith, *Mon Père*,
nor do I hanker after consolations. (The sky

is just an atmospheric trick; my glass is full
of vinegar that stings the throat, the eye;

each canticle is so much foolishness.) I pray
a novena of stripped-back petition, beg

for nothing more than scattered mustard seed.
My tastes have dwindled down to a dry bud,

but I have found that bitter things are good—
and microscopic seeds are more than food.

89

I am content to huddle
in this cloud—did not God

permit the morning mist
to thicken, and wrap around

his body like a shroud?—
there is no nourishment

in irritable facts. But I sense
that fogginess has its own glory—

that charcoal and thurible serve
to perform the cloud's story.

90

How do small birds weather the storms? Even their silence is testament, under the eaves, under the weighed-down boughs. Each raindrop is a brutal bounty. I listen and listen for the sun.

91

Here is a list of kisses I have given:
Rose with her tough-skinned love.

Papa, silver-bearded patriarch.
Mama in her coffin, small and cold.

Fulsome Marie. Cool-headed Pauline,
bright Céline and Léonie the lost.

You, *Mon Père,* received your only kiss
from my lips as a golden-haired child.

The Pope himself, his fingers dry and frail.
Then Carmel. Its kaleidoscope of kisses;

each with their sisterly bittersweet gloss—
suffering coated in hope's hard shell.

In my breathlessness, I kissed it all:
the wooden bowl, the purple stole,

the clutch of fallen flowers;
the cross—the cross.

92

I write what I want to believe,
I cherish what makes me recoil,
I smile at the gifts that mean nothing,
I stumble—this lamp has no oil.

I bite my lip when others take
my thoughts. I bless the cold.
At Compline, I sense I am dancing;
a novice, I feel I am old.

I see no reason and I taste no fruit,
I have no dreams and do not understand.
I sit at the table of sinners, waiting
for bread with empty hands.

93

I used to imagine my name was written in the stars. I only had to raise my hand and point to feel all heaven flowing in my veins. Now I all but forget to look; I am concerned only with the flowers in my arms, and to whom I may give them.

94

Language eludes me, *Mon Père.*
I once believed words could be moved

like beads in my chaplet of practices,
each deed, each sacrifice, given its due.

Now I find words are like water—
lucent, but borderless; seeping

and pooling in strange hinterlands.
It is language that writes me—every

attempt to slip out of it leaves me
here, on the silent white sand.

95

I write what I want to believe,
I write—   what—
I want to believe—
I write
                    what I want
I want to believe
                              I write
what I want—   to believe I write
what I want
        to believe I write
what I   want to
I believe I write—

what I believe,   I believe
        what I write, I write
                what I write, I want
        what I believe I want—
I write   to believe
        I want to write
I believe I want to believe

to want to write to what—
to believe—

96

There is no way of repaying love, and love by its nature does not seek repayment. What then of the calls for sacrifice and prayer? We are like children—including you, *Mon Père*—for we must borrow even the means to offer our little gifts and cards.

Every time I play my part, I am returning what has been lent. Every breath I draw, I return to the sky. But even children can plead a cause, can call for help and save a soul. I am filling the loan of the evening with my written intercessions. Soon they will all be folded up, ready to send.

97

When you have whittled away at the shell of the soul, you get to a point where precious little is left—translucent nacre, the size of a fingernail. The wall between time and eternity worn luminously thin.

In the same way I am barely aware of the difference between suffering and joy. Such wisps of contingency are nothing more than the soft cry of a dove.

98

Mon Père, I am ~~enamored~~

~~bloodied~~   ~~torqued~~   ~~a little child~~

~~a bright design   a painted saint~~

reduced to a small
                              token
~~a dazzled bird~~
~~a patch of moss~~
a lost
grain ~~of sugar~~
~~of rice~~
of sand

in me there is no longer ~~infinity~~
~~a span of years~~
~~a holy week~~
the clutch of seconds necessary
        for the Darlot lens

I cannot
~~lift my arms~~   ~~my eyes~~
                scatter

                                any more
~~petals~~
~~letters~~
~~blessings~~
shreds of hope I

barely catch my ragdoll breath barely

still
~~my beating heart~~

99

I will not look down—I will come down. So swift, I will be quicker than my own poor name; so close, you will be further from your shadow than from me; so quiet I can hide behind your own caught breath.

100

When the scroll of my life
is unfurled, *Mon Père*,

you will read a fifth gospel—
of how a girl crept to the stable

with grit on her feet
and her eyes on the stars—

of how she was given
the bitterest bread at the table

and wrapped herself up
in the luminous dark.

Afterword

These poems are not intended to provide a straightforward biography of Thérèse. My earlier collection, *Thérèse: Poems* (Paraclete, 2020) did take a more clearly biographical approach. The poems in *This Transfigured Chapel of the Threads* are each sparked by some image, fact or phrase drawn from Thérèse's life and thought, but while they are structured in a loosely chronological order, I was more concerned to explore how far imagery and language could encapsulate and elaborate on those initial sparks.

Ideally the poems stand without historical or biographical context. However, while not strictly necessary, readers might like to acquaint themselves with Thérèse and her spirituality by consulting some of the titles listed in the *Resources* section.

In case it's helpful, I've also included the following slightly fuller biographical sketch, providing indicative poem numbers from this collection where a little information may give the reader a steer, although all the poems here have thoughts and directions of their own, beyond any immediate context:

Thérèse Martin (1873–97) was the youngest surviving daughter (3) of Louis and Zélie Martin. She developed an affinity for mental prayer and contemplation at an early age (1, 2, 5, 6) and entered the Carmelite monastery at Lisieux in 1888, having petitioned her early admittance with the Pope (7, 11, 12, 13). The pilgrimage she and her father and sister took to Rome allowed her some experience of travel (8), and of what she saw as worldly behavior (9) and the needs of priests (10). In Carmel, she developed a spirituality of humility (19, 29, 36, 44, 45), compassion (34) and confidence in God's love and mercy (56), somewhat at odds with the prevailing ethos of penance and appeasing God's judgment (72). While her ambitions to do God's work were vast (21, 33, 65, 84) including a longing to have been a priest herself (74), she found her ultimate vocation to be one of love at the heart of the Church. She cherished little acts of care and kindness (22, 42, 69), even for those she disliked (62), while struggling increasingly with ill-health (61, 76, 77) and spiritual doubt (60, 88, 89) herself. She and her sister Carmelites were briefly taken in by a fake persona concocted by the malicious hoaxer, Léo Taxil (73). But this did not put Thérèse off praying for and even considering herself no better than sinners and atheists (82). She continued to write to her spiritual director until the end of her life (47, 59, 75), although he seldom replied (83), and all her letters to him have been lost. Thérèse died in 1897 of tuberculosis, sensing that her life and mission were not over (79, 81, 99, 100).

Thérèse had painted a little (52), and was a talented writer (46), penning poems (40), letters (87) and a memoir of her life. In the same monastery, her sister Céline developed her own talents as a painter and photographer (71). In addition, two other, older blood sisters, Pauline and Marie, and a cousin, another Marie, were Carmelite nuns at the same monastery, and after Thérèse's death, they cherished her memory and supported the cause for her sanctity. She was canonized in 1925 and made a Doctor of the Church in 1997.

Resources

Other Thérèse-inspired texts by Sarah Law

Readers may be interested in my own previous creative work inspired by Thérèse, each of which takes a different approach and style. These are:

Law, Sarah. *Thérèse: Poems*. Brewster MA: Paraclete, 2020.
———. *Sketches from a Sunlit Heaven: A Novel*. Eugene, Oregon: Wipf and Stock, 2022.

There are many resources on Thérèse's life and legacy. I am especially indebted to the following:

Websites

The online archive of the Carmel of Lisieux. http://www.archives-carmel-lisieux.fr/english/carmel/index.php/accueil-home
Thérèse of Lisieux: A Gateway. http://www.thereseoflisieux.org/

Nonfiction

Görres, Ida Friederike. *The Hidden Face: A Study of St. Thérèse of Lisieux*. Translated by Richard and Clara Winston. San Francisco: Ignatius, 2003.
Kochiss, Joseph P. *A Companion to Saint Thérèse of Lisieux: Her Life and Work & The People and Places in Her Story*. Brooklyn, NY: Angelico, 2014.
Moorcroft, Jennifer. *Saint Thérèse of Lisieux and Her Sisters*. Leominster, UK: Gracewing, 2003.

Nevin, Thomas R. *Thérèse of Lisieux: God's Gentle Warrior.* Oxford, UK: Oxford University Press, 2006.

————. *The Last Years of Saint Thérèse: Doubt and Darkness, 1895–1897.* New York: Oxford University Press, 2013.

Udris John. *Holy Daring: The Fearless Trust of Saint Thérèse of Lisieux.* Leominster, UK: Gracewing, 1997.

Films

Cavalier, Alain. *Thérèse.* 1986.

www.ingramcontent.com/pod-product-compliance
Lightning Source LLC
Chambersburg PA
CBHW070826100426
42813CB00003B/508